EMMANUEL JOSEPH

The Power Map, How Billionaires Influence Countries, Policies, and Global Progress

Copyright © 2025 by Emmanuel Joseph

All rights reserved. No part of this publication may be reproduced, stored or transmitted in any form or by any means, electronic, mechanical, photocopying, recording, scanning, or otherwise without written permission from the publisher. It is illegal to copy this book, post it to a website, or distribute it by any other means without permission.

First edition

This book was professionally typeset on Reedsy.
Find out more at reedsy.com

Contents

1	Chapter 1: The Rise of the Billionaire Class	1
2	Chapter 2: The Political Power of Billionaires	3
3	Chapter 3: Economic Influence and Market Manipulation	5
4	Chapter 4: Billionaire Philanthropy and Social Change	7
5	Chapter 5: The Media Moguls	9
6	Chapter 6: Technology Titans	10
7	Chapter 7: Energy and Environmental Influence	11
8	Chapter 8: Education and Intellectual Capital	12
9	Chapter 9: Healthcare and Medical Advancements	13
10	Chapter 10: The Role of Billionaires in Global Trade	14
11	Chapter 11: Cultural Influence and the Arts	15
12	Chapter 12: The Influence of Billionaires on Infrastructure...	16
13	Chapter 13: Billionaires and Innovation	17
14	Chapter 14: The Ethical Dilemmas of Billionaire Influence	18
15	Chapter 15: The Impact on Democracy	19
16	Chapter 16: Global Governance and the Role of Billionaires	20
17	Chapter 17: The Future of Billionaire Influence	21
18	Chapter 18: Billionaires and Social Media Influence	22
19	Chapter 19: The Billionaire Lifestyle and its Cultural...	23
20	Chapter 20: The Dark Side of Billionaire Influence	24
21	Chapter 21: Grassroots Movements and Billionaire Opposition	25
22	Chapter 22: The Psychology of Billionaire Success	26

1

Chapter 1: The Rise of the Billionaire Class

In the past few decades, the world has seen an unprecedented accumulation of wealth in the hands of a select few. These billionaires have not only amassed fortunes but have also gained significant power and influence over global affairs. This chapter explores the historical context and socio-economic factors that have led to the emergence of the billionaire class. From the industrial revolution to the digital age, we delve into the key events and innovations that have enabled individuals to accumulate such vast wealth.

The concentration of wealth in the hands of billionaires raises questions about economic inequality and the implications for democracy. We examine how billionaires leverage their financial resources to shape policies and influence political decisions. By funding political campaigns, lobbying for favorable regulations, and establishing philanthropic foundations, billionaires have become powerful actors in the global arena. This chapter highlights the ways in which their influence extends beyond their immediate business interests to impact societal norms and values.

The rise of the billionaire class is also a reflection of broader economic trends, such as globalization and technological advancements. We explore how these trends have created opportunities for wealth creation while exacerbating disparities between the rich and the poor. By analyzing case studies of prominent billionaires, we gain insights into the strategies they employ to maintain and expand their influence. This chapter sets the stage for understanding the complex dynamics between wealth, power, and global progress.

2

Chapter 2: The Political Power of Billionaires

Billionaires wield considerable political power, often shaping policies and decisions that affect millions of people. This chapter delves into the mechanisms through which billionaires exert their influence on the political landscape. From campaign contributions to direct involvement in governance, we explore the various avenues through which billionaires impact political outcomes. By examining the role of money in politics, we uncover the ways in which wealth translates into political power.

The relationship between billionaires and politicians is often symbiotic, with both parties benefiting from mutual support. We investigate how billionaires use their resources to gain access to key decision-makers and shape policy agendas. Through lobbying, think tanks, and strategic alliances, billionaires can push for policies that align with their interests. This chapter provides a nuanced understanding of the ethical considerations and potential conflicts of interest that arise from such relationships.

Political power is not limited to national boundaries; billionaires also play a significant role in shaping international relations. We explore how billionaires influence global governance through organizations such as the World Economic Forum and philanthropic initiatives. By examining the impact of billionaire philanthropy on global issues such as health, education, and climate change, we gain insights into the ways in which their influence extends beyond traditional political arenas. This chapter highlights the interconnectedness of wealth, power, and global progress.

3

Chapter 3: Economic Influence and Market Manipulation

Billionaires have the ability to shape markets and economic trends through their investments and business decisions. This chapter examines the economic influence of billionaires and the ways in which they can manipulate markets to their advantage. From stock market fluctuations to real estate developments, we explore the impact of billionaire actions on the global economy. By analyzing case studies of market manipulation, we uncover the tactics used by billionaires to maintain their financial dominance.

The economic influence of billionaires extends beyond their individual investments to shape broader market trends. We investigate how billionaires drive innovation and economic growth through their entrepreneurial ventures. By funding startups, acquiring companies, and investing in new technologies, billionaires play a pivotal role in shaping the future of industries. This chapter highlights the positive contributions of billionaire influence while also examining the potential risks and challenges associated with market concentration.

Market manipulation by billionaires can have far-reaching consequences for ordinary people and the global economy. We explore the ethical implications of such actions and the regulatory frameworks designed to mitigate the risks. By examining the role of financial institutions, government oversight, and international cooperation, we gain a comprehensive understanding of the mechanisms that govern market behavior. This chapter provides a critical analysis of the balance between economic freedom and regulatory intervention in the context of billionaire influence.

4

Chapter 4: Billionaire Philanthropy and Social Change

Billionaires often engage in philanthropic activities, using their wealth to address social issues and drive positive change. This chapter explores the motivations behind billionaire philanthropy and the impact of their charitable initiatives. From funding education and healthcare programs to supporting environmental sustainability, we examine the diverse ways in which billionaires contribute to societal well-being. By analyzing the effectiveness of philanthropic efforts, we gain insights into the potential for meaningful social change.

The motivations behind billionaire philanthropy can vary, ranging from altruism to strategic interests. We investigate the personal and professional factors that drive billionaires to engage in charitable activities. By examining the impact of billionaire philanthropy on public perceptions and social norms, we uncover the ways in which their actions shape societal values. This chapter highlights the complex interplay between wealth, power, and social responsibility.

Billionaire philanthropy also raises questions about accountability and transparency. We explore the mechanisms through which philanthropic organizations are held accountable for their actions and the challenges associated with measuring impact. By examining case studies of successful and controversial philanthropic initiatives, we gain a nuanced understanding of the potential benefits and limitations of billionaire philanthropy. This chapter provides a critical analysis of the role of philanthropy in driving social change and addressing global challenges.

5

Chapter 5: The Media Moguls

In today's world, media is a powerful tool that shapes public opinion and influences societal norms. This chapter delves into the role of billionaires in the media industry and how they use their ownership and control of media outlets to influence public perception. From traditional newspapers to digital platforms, we explore the ways in which billionaires leverage media to amplify their voices and agendas. By examining the strategies employed by media moguls, we gain insights into the power dynamics within the media landscape.

The consolidation of media ownership in the hands of a few billionaires raises concerns about the diversity and independence of journalism. We investigate the potential risks associated with media monopolies and the impact on democratic discourse. By analyzing case studies of media moguls and their influence on news coverage, we uncover the ways in which billionaire interests shape the information that reaches the public. This chapter highlights the critical role of media in shaping societal values and the ethical considerations surrounding media ownership.

6

Chapter 6: Technology Titans

The technology sector has been a major driver of economic growth and innovation, and billionaires in this industry wield significant influence over the future of technology. This chapter explores the role of tech billionaires in shaping technological advancements and the impact of their innovations on society. From artificial intelligence to space exploration, we examine the visionary projects and initiatives led by technology titans. By analyzing the strategies and philosophies of tech billionaires, we gain insights into the ways in which they envision and shape the future.

The influence of technology billionaires extends beyond their companies to affect broader societal trends. We investigate how tech billionaires use their resources to influence education, policy, and social norms. By funding research institutions, advocating for regulatory changes, and promoting technological literacy, tech billionaires play a pivotal role in shaping the discourse around technology and its implications. This chapter provides a nuanced understanding of the complex relationship between technology, power, and global progress.

7

Chapter 7: Energy and Environmental Influence

Billionaires in the energy sector have a profound impact on global environmental policies and sustainability efforts. This chapter delves into the role of energy billionaires in shaping the future of energy production and consumption. From fossil fuels to renewable energy, we explore the ways in which billionaires influence the transition to sustainable energy sources. By examining the strategies employed by energy tycoons, we gain insights into the challenges and opportunities associated with achieving environmental sustainability.

The influence of energy billionaires extends to global environmental governance and climate policy. We investigate how billionaires use their resources to advocate for environmental regulations, fund conservation initiatives, and support research on climate change. By analyzing case studies of energy billionaires and their contributions to environmental sustainability, we uncover the ways in which their actions shape the global response to environmental challenges. This chapter highlights the interconnectedness of energy, wealth, and environmental progress.

8

Chapter 8: Education and Intellectual Capital

Billionaires have a significant impact on the field of education and the development of intellectual capital. This chapter explores the role of billionaires in shaping educational policies, funding institutions, and promoting innovative approaches to learning. From funding scholarships to establishing research universities, we examine the diverse ways in which billionaires contribute to the advancement of education. By analyzing the motivations and strategies behind their philanthropic efforts, we gain insights into the potential for meaningful educational change.

The influence of billionaires on education extends to shaping the discourse around knowledge and intellectual capital. We investigate how billionaires use their resources to support research, promote intellectual freedom, and advocate for policy changes in education. By examining case studies of educational philanthropy, we uncover the ways in which billionaire initiatives drive innovation and address educational disparities. This chapter provides a critical analysis of the role of billionaires in shaping the future of education and intellectual progress.

9

Chapter 9: Healthcare and Medical Advancements

The healthcare sector is a critical area where billionaires can have a significant impact on global well-being. This chapter delves into the role of billionaires in advancing medical research, funding healthcare initiatives, and addressing public health challenges. From supporting vaccine development to funding healthcare infrastructure, we explore the diverse ways in which billionaires contribute to improving healthcare outcomes. By analyzing the effectiveness of their initiatives, we gain insights into the potential for transformative change in the healthcare sector.

Billionaire influence in healthcare extends to shaping health policy and advocating for global health initiatives. We investigate how billionaires use their resources to support research institutions, promote public health campaigns, and advocate for policy changes in healthcare. By examining case studies of billionaire philanthropy in healthcare, we uncover the ways in which their actions contribute to addressing global health challenges. This chapter highlights the critical role of billionaires in driving medical advancements and improving global health.

10

Chapter 10: The Role of Billionaires in Global Trade

Global trade is a complex system that billionaires significantly influence through their investments and business ventures. This chapter examines the role of billionaires in shaping international trade policies and economic relations between countries. From trade agreements to multinational corporations, we explore the ways in which billionaires drive global commerce and impact economic development. By analyzing case studies of billionaire-led companies, we gain insights into the strategies they employ to navigate and shape the global market.

The influence of billionaires in global trade extends to shaping trade regulations and economic policies. We investigate how billionaires use their resources to advocate for trade policies that benefit their interests and promote free market principles. By examining the impact of billionaire influence on trade relations between countries, we uncover the ways in which their actions shape the global economic landscape. This chapter highlights the interconnectedness of wealth, trade, and global progress.

11

Chapter 11: Cultural Influence and the Arts

Billionaires often have a profound impact on the cultural sector, shaping the arts, entertainment, and cultural heritage. This chapter delves into the role of billionaires in supporting and promoting cultural initiatives. From funding museums and art galleries to producing films and supporting creative industries, we explore the diverse ways in which billionaires contribute to cultural enrichment. By analyzing the motivations behind their cultural patronage, we gain insights into the potential for positive cultural impact.

The influence of billionaires on culture extends to shaping public perceptions and societal values. We investigate how billionaires use their resources to promote cultural projects that align with their personal and ideological beliefs. By examining case studies of billionaire-sponsored cultural initiatives, we uncover the ways in which their actions shape cultural discourse and influence artistic trends. This chapter provides a critical analysis of the role of billionaires in driving cultural progress and preserving cultural heritage.

12

Chapter 12: The Influence of Billionaires on Infrastructure Development

Infrastructure development is a critical area where billionaires can have a significant impact on economic growth and societal well-being. This chapter explores the role of billionaires in funding and supporting infrastructure projects, from transportation systems to urban development. By examining the strategies and motivations behind billionaire investments in infrastructure, we gain insights into the potential for transformative change in this sector.

The influence of billionaires on infrastructure development extends to shaping public policies and regulatory frameworks. We investigate how billionaires use their resources to advocate for infrastructure projects that align with their interests and promote sustainable development. By analyzing case studies of successful infrastructure initiatives led by billionaires, we uncover the ways in which their actions contribute to economic development and societal progress. This chapter highlights the interconnectedness of wealth, infrastructure, and global progress.

13

Chapter 13: Billionaires and Innovation

Innovation is a key driver of economic growth and societal progress, and billionaires play a pivotal role in fostering innovation. This chapter delves into the ways in which billionaires support and promote innovative ideas and technologies. From funding research and development to supporting startups and entrepreneurs, we explore the diverse ways in which billionaires contribute to the innovation ecosystem. By analyzing the strategies and motivations behind their support for innovation, we gain insights into the potential for transformative change.

The influence of billionaires on innovation extends to shaping the future of industries and technological advancements. We investigate how billionaires use their resources to drive innovation and promote disruptive technologies. By examining case studies of successful innovations led by billionaires, we uncover the ways in which their actions contribute to economic growth and societal progress. This chapter provides a critical analysis of the role of billionaires in driving innovation and shaping the future.

14

Chapter 14: The Ethical Dilemmas of Billionaire Influence

The influence of billionaires on global affairs raises important ethical questions and dilemmas. This chapter explores the ethical considerations surrounding billionaire influence and the potential risks and challenges associated with their power. From conflicts of interest to issues of accountability and transparency, we examine the complex ethical landscape in which billionaires operate. By analyzing case studies of ethical dilemmas faced by billionaires, we gain insights into the potential for both positive and negative impacts on society.

The ethical dilemmas of billionaire influence extend to questions of fairness and justice. We investigate how the concentration of wealth and power in the hands of a few can exacerbate social inequalities and undermine democratic processes. By examining the role of regulatory frameworks and oversight mechanisms, we uncover the ways in which society can address these ethical challenges and promote responsible billionaire influence. This chapter provides a nuanced understanding of the ethical implications of wealth and power in the global arena.

15

Chapter 15: The Impact on Democracy

The concentration of wealth and power in the hands of billionaires raises important questions about the health of democratic institutions. This chapter explores the impact of billionaire influence on democratic processes and governance. From campaign financing to media ownership, we examine the ways in which billionaires can shape political outcomes and public opinion. By analyzing the potential risks and challenges associated with their influence, we gain insights into the implications for democratic accountability and representation.

The impact of billionaire influence on democracy extends to issues of transparency and accountability. We investigate how the actions of billionaires can undermine public trust in democratic institutions and processes. By examining case studies of billionaire involvement in politics and governance, we uncover the ways in which their influence can both support and challenge democratic norms. This chapter provides a critical analysis of the role of billionaires in shaping the future of democracy.

16

Chapter 16: Global Governance and the Role of Billionaires

Billionaires are increasingly playing a role in global governance, influencing international organizations and policy-making processes. This chapter delves into the ways in which billionaires contribute to shaping global governance structures and addressing transnational challenges. From participation in global forums to funding international initiatives, we explore the diverse ways in which billionaires impact global governance. By analyzing the strategies and motivations behind their involvement, we gain insights into the potential for positive and negative effects on global progress.

The role of billionaires in global governance extends to addressing issues such as climate change, global health, and economic development. We investigate how billionaires use their resources to support international cooperation and promote global solutions to complex challenges. By examining case studies of successful and controversial global initiatives led by billionaires, we uncover the ways in which their actions shape the future of global governance. This chapter highlights the interconnectedness of wealth, power, and global progress on the international stage.

17

Chapter 17: The Future of Billionaire Influence

As we look to the future, the influence of billionaires on global affairs is likely to continue evolving. This chapter explores the potential future trends and challenges associated with billionaire influence. From the impact of technological advancements to changing societal values, we examine the factors that will shape the role of billionaires in the years to come. By analyzing potential scenarios and trends, we gain insights into the ways in which billionaire influence will continue to impact global progress.

The future of billionaire influence also raises important questions about the balance between economic freedom and regulatory oversight. We investigate the potential for new regulatory frameworks and oversight mechanisms to address the risks and challenges associated with billionaire influence. By examining the role of civil society, governments, and international organizations, we uncover the ways in which society can promote responsible and ethical billionaire influence. This chapter provides a forward-looking perspective on the evolving dynamics of wealth, power, and global progress.

18

Chapter 18: Billionaires and Social Media Influence

Social media platforms have become powerful tools for communication and influence, and billionaires in the tech industry often own or control these platforms. This chapter explores the role of billionaires in shaping social media landscapes and the impact of their actions on public discourse. From content moderation to algorithmic changes, we examine the ways in which billionaires influence what we see and share on social media. By analyzing case studies of social media giants, we gain insights into the power dynamics within the digital world.

The influence of billionaires on social media extends to issues of privacy, free speech, and misinformation. We investigate how billionaires navigate the challenges of regulating content while balancing user rights and corporate interests. By examining the ethical considerations and potential risks associated with social media influence, we uncover the ways in which billionaire actions shape the digital public sphere. This chapter highlights the critical role of social media in shaping societal values and the ethical implications of digital power.

19

Chapter 19: The Billionaire Lifestyle and its Cultural Impact

The lifestyles of billionaires often capture public fascination and can have a significant cultural impact. This chapter delves into the ways in which billionaire lifestyles shape societal aspirations and consumer behavior. From luxury brands to exclusive experiences, we explore the influence of billionaires on fashion, travel, and entertainment. By analyzing the portrayal of billionaires in media and popular culture, we gain insights into the cultural narratives that surround wealth and success.

The cultural impact of billionaire lifestyles extends to shaping social norms and values. We investigate how the visibility of billionaire wealth affects public perceptions of success and ambition. By examining the role of luxury industries and marketing strategies, we uncover the ways in which billionaire lifestyles influence consumer behavior and societal trends. This chapter provides a critical analysis of the cultural dynamics of wealth and the implications for social aspirations and identity.

20

Chapter 20: The Dark Side of Billionaire Influence

While billionaires can drive positive change, their influence also has potential downsides and controversies. This chapter explores the darker aspects of billionaire influence, from exploitation and corruption to environmental degradation and labor abuses. By examining case studies of controversial billionaires and their actions, we gain insights into the potential negative impacts of concentrated wealth and power. This chapter provides a balanced perspective on the risks and challenges associated with billionaire influence.

The dark side of billionaire influence extends to issues of accountability and justice. We investigate how regulatory frameworks and legal mechanisms address the unethical actions of billionaires. By examining the role of whistleblowers, investigative journalism, and civil society, we uncover the ways in which society can hold billionaires accountable for their actions. This chapter highlights the importance of transparency and oversight in mitigating the negative impacts of billionaire influence.

21

Chapter 21: Grassroots Movements and Billionaire Opposition

Grassroots movements and civil society organizations often challenge the influence of billionaires and advocate for social and economic justice. This chapter delves into the role of grassroots movements in opposing and countering billionaire influence. From labor unions to environmental activists, we explore the diverse ways in which ordinary people organize and mobilize against concentrated wealth and power. By analyzing case studies of successful grassroots movements, we gain insights into the strategies and tactics used to challenge billionaire influence.

The opposition to billionaire influence extends to issues of policy advocacy and public awareness. We investigate how grassroots movements use media, social networks, and public campaigns to raise awareness and drive change. By examining the impact of grassroots activism on policy decisions and societal values, we uncover the ways in which ordinary people can influence global progress. This chapter provides a critical analysis of the power dynamics between billionaires and grassroots movements.

22

Chapter 22: The Psychology of Billionaire Success

Understanding the psychology behind billionaire success can provide valuable insights into the motivations and behaviors that drive their influence. This chapter explores the psychological traits and characteristics commonly found among billionaires. From risk-taking and resilience to vision and leadership, we examine the attributes that contribute to their success. By analyzing psychological research and case studies of prominent billionaires, we gain insights into the mindsets that shape their actions and decisions.

The psychology of billionaire success extends to understanding the impact of wealth on individual well-being and behavior. We investigate how the accumulation of wealth affects personal identity, relationships, and values. By examining the challenges and dilemmas faced by billionaires, we uncover the ways in which their psychological traits influence their interactions with the world. This chapter provides a nuanced understanding of the human aspects of billionaire influence and the complexities of their success.

"The Power Map: How Billionaires Influence Countries, Policies, and Global Progress":

In a world where wealth and power are increasingly concentrated in the hands of a few, "The Power Map" takes you on a captivating journey through

CHAPTER 22: THE PSYCHOLOGY OF BILLIONAIRE SUCCESS

the corridors of influence and control. This insightful book unravels the intricate web of billionaires who shape countries, steer policies, and drive global progress.

From the rise of the billionaire class to their profound impact on democracy, economics, and innovation, "The Power Map" provides an in-depth analysis of how these elite individuals leverage their fortunes to mold our world. Discover the strategies behind their political clout, the ethical dilemmas they face, and the role they play in addressing critical global challenges such as climate change, healthcare, and education.

Through compelling case studies and thought-provoking insights, this book reveals the multifaceted ways in which billionaires wield their power—whether through philanthropy, media ownership, or technological advancements. It sheds light on their motivations, their successes, and the controversies that surround them.

"The Power Map" is an essential read for anyone interested in understanding the complex interplay between wealth, power, and societal progress. As we look to the future, this book provides a forward-looking perspective on the evolving dynamics of billionaire influence and offers a critical analysis of what this means for our world.

www.ingramcontent.com/pod-product-compliance
Lightning Source LLC
LaVergne TN
LVHW010445070526
838199LV00066B/6197